CAN YOU NOT WATCH WITH ME ONE HOUR?

HOW TO GET FREE AND STAY FREE

JOSHUA FLYNN

LCCN: 024921022

Copyright Case I'D: 1-14303805661

E-Book: 978-1-304-25179-4

Paperback: 978-1-304-25177-0

Hardcover: 978-1-304-25175-6

TABLE OF CONTENTS

Main Testimony v

Sinners Prayer viii

Testimony x

Prayer To This Day 1

Prayer Testimony# 1 5

Decree And Declare Prayer 6

Testimony # 2 7

Prayers For Immorality 8

Testimony# 3 10

Prayer For Hearing And Seeing God's Signs 11

Testimony# 4 12

Prayer To Stay In The Will Of God 14

Testimony# 5 16

Prayer To Ascend God's Holy Hill 18

Testimony# 6 20

Prayer Of Declarations To Start Your Day 22

Testimony# 7 24

Prayer For Deliverance 26

Testimony# 8 29

Prayer To Change Spiritual Smell 31

Testimony# 9 32

Prayer to Exalt My Horn 34

Testimony# 10 36

Prayer To Keep Lamp Burning 38

Testimony# 11 39

Prayer To Speak Life Over Yourself 41

Testimony# 12 43

Prayer To Open Your Spiritual Eyes 45

Testimony# 13 47

Prayer For Healing 49

Testimony# 14 51

Prayer Against Evil Embargos 53

Testimony# 15 55

Enough Is Enough Prayer 57

Testimony# 16 59

Prayer For Demonic Headaches 60

Testimony# 17 63

Prayer For Healing Upon Yourself 65

Testimony# 18 68

Prayer For Unclean Spirits 70

Testimony# 19 72

Prayer For forbid going back to the old me. 74

Testimony# 20 76

Main Testimony

Even as I committed my life to the streets and its troubles for more than 18 years, I have always considered myself a person of faith, one who knew about God and even prayed occasionally in extreme distress. But it wasn't until I fully submitted my issues to God in prayer, that I began to understand the true power of prayer to transform my life from addictions, mindsets and a host of strongholds, to one forever changed and sold out for Jesus.

A few years ago, I faced a difficult period where I felt lost and was unsure of my path. I was in jail dealing with multiple addictions, unforgiveness, lust, and bitterness to name a few. Despite my efforts, I couldn't find a solution or a pathway out. Feeling overwhelmed and alone, I turned to prayer as my last resort and in those moments of vulnerability and full submission. I realized that I wanted and needed God. I only knew how to reach God through prayer. I needed a prayer that would speak to the depths of my heart and soul. As I allowed myself to entertain my longing for change, an overwhelming need to connect with God himself led me to write a prayer that has since become a cornerstone of my spiritual journey.

Writing the prayer was an incredibly transformative experience. As I put pen to paper, I felt a sense of peace and clarity that I had never experienced before. The words flowed naturally, each line reflecting my deepest hopes, fears, and desires. It was, as if God was guiding my hand, helping me articulate what I could not ever express before.

Since I prayed this prayer, my life has changed in remarkable ways. I have experienced a sense of inner peace and strength that has helped me navigate through my daily challenges. There have been moments of unexpected blessings and support that I can only attribute to the power of this prayer. Friends and family who have joined me in this prayer have also shared their stories of hope and renewal, and experienced supernatural encounters through unexpected encounters with others.

Through this prayer, my faith has deepened, and my relationship with God has become more personal and profound. I have learned to trust God's timing and to seek His guidance in every aspect of my life. This prayer continues to be a source of comfort and inspiration, reminding me of God's unwavering presence and love.

If You feel like you have tried everything you could your way, and you have not had any success, then that is the beginning of your transformation, because you have to get tired of doing things your way first. Because in order for God to be able to step in and help you, he must be able to affect your heart first. Because in this madness of doing it our way, GOD cannot work on our behalf because of our free will! The second step is: you just raise your hands and surrender to GOD, ask him to forgive you and take away whatever is bringing you down. There is so much power in surrender. So, let God have your weakness and pain. The Reason is because his strength is made perfect in your weakness. This is when you die to yourself, and when you die to yourself, then you come to know yourself, and when you come to know yourself, and who you are, which means that if you give your life to Christ and repent and get baptized, you will then become a son or daughter of the living GOD. Then you will begin to truly live. But, if you don't repent, and you want to cling to your life, and what you have, you, will not come to know yourself and as a result, you will continue to Live in Poverty. And it will be you that will be in poverty. At this point even what you have will be taken away, and you will loose your life! Regardless of what the enemy told you in the past, and even now, it is never too late to surrender! If you decide today, you will repent which means you turn away from sin, your life will never be the same! The next step is read this prayer listed below out loud over yourself, surrender your past and allow this day to be the first day of the rest of your life. Your life will never be the same. I decree and I declare in the name of Jesus that as you read this prayer and believe it, you will receive healing and redemption! This prayer has been a beacon of hope and a testament to the power of faith. I am profoundly grateful for the spiritual growth and the divine connection it has fostered in my life. I encourage anyone facing big or small challenges to embrace the power of prayer, for it has the ability to transform our hearts and lives in unimaginable ways.

Sinners Prayer

In the name of Jesus, I come to you right now and I repent! I lay this life at your feet, and I surrender! I say to you God, I have lived as a sinner. I have been hurt and I hurt others and I've hurt myself. Lord, I forgive those who hurt me, please forgive me. I ask you right now to wash me in your blood and forgive me of my sins. I receive your sacrifice for my life, and I ask you to be my Savior. Come and be my Lord, come be my best friend, come live your life through me Lord Jesus. Today, I answer the call. I believe in you that you are the son of God. I believe that you have died for me, and I believe that you rose again on the third day for my justification. Right now, I receive Jesus into my heart as my savior, as my Lord and as my king. Lord, help me break the chains of the enemy over my life now in Jesus' name. Deliver me and set me free I decree and declare that the power of sin, Satan, or hell or the grave is broken over my life even now in JESUS Name! From today on I am a child of God and I go forward forever and never backward. Father, thank you thank you for this harvest of my precious soul and I thank you because only you are able to save me and your precious people through me. I have come to you based on the authority of scripture and I decree, and I declare my sins are forgiven. I decree and I declare in Jesus name that I am a recipient of the life of Jesus from today on the power of sin, Satan, hell and the grave is broken over my life. I go forward forever, and backward never. Change my heart so that I crave you, Lord, above all. Spirit of our God, Father, Son and Holy Spirit, Most Holy Trinity, descend upon me now. Please purify me, mold me, fill me with You, and use me. Banish all the forces of evil from me; destroy them and vanquish them so that I can be healthy and do good deeds.

In Jesus Name, banish from me all curses, hexes, spells, witchcraft, black magic, demonic assignments, malefice and the evil eye; diabolic infestations, oppressions, possessions; all that is evil and sinful, jealousy, treachery, envy; all physical, psychological, moral, spiritual and diabolical ailments; as well as all enticing spirits, deaf, dumb, blind, mute and sleeping spirits, new-age spirits, occult spirits, religious spirits, antichrist spirits, and any other spirits of death and darkness. In the name of Jesus Christ, it is so! Thank You Thank You Thank You!

This prayer was the beginning of many prayers. As I committed myself to an hour of prayer daily, God began his great work in me, and he will not let me fail.

GOD pulled me out of the mud of addiction and sin and gave me my life's purpose! So, I have been charged to help teach others how to get out of the mud of addiction and sin and stay out for good. I decree and I declare in JESUS name If you recognize what is in your sight, then that which is hidden from you will become plain to you. For there is nothing hidden which will not become manifest."

I need to say how delighted I am to be here, where I can hopefully reach many people who will relate to my story and begin to feel the urge to rise up and with God's help, take back control of any area of their life where they may have fallen short! I would like to take you all on a journey of my deliverance as much as my memory will allow, about where I was, and even where I am right now because of the Grace Of GOD! If You Learn the Way to Suffer Then You Will Gain Power Over You Suffering! You Have to Know What or Who You Are Fighting to Be Able to Defeat Them.

TESTIMONY

Hi, my name is Joshua, Yahweh pulled me out of the mud of addiction and sin and gave my life purpose! So, I have been charged to help teach others how to get out of the mud of addiction and sin and stay out for good!

I need not pause to say how very delighted I am to be here where I can hopefully reach many people who will relate to my story and feel the urge to rise up and take back control of any area of their life where they may have fallen short! I would like to take you all on a mental trek, as long as memory chords will lengthen about where I was and where I am right now because of the grace of God! if you learn the way to suffer then you will gain power over your sufferings!

A wise woman once said that you have to know what or who you are fighting to be able to defeat them." There was a boy who grew up in a Christian home, the baby of 10 siblings out of which (9) survived, he used to go to church every Sunday morning and night, he was very crafty and full of spark he heard about who God was and what Jesus did from a pretty early age but didn't quite understand it enough to take it seriously!

Between the age gap, his brothers going to the military, and he himself being stuck at home with four sisters, they often fought or argued! He felt unnoticed when they moved into the city. He began to look for friends on his street. The church taught that you should not have a television and you should not have tattoos and pierce your ears as a guy because your body is the lord's temple. So, he felt estranged and indifferent to the guys in the neighborhood who picked on him because of his different appearance and the way he carried himself! God was always in his life, but he didn't fully know this to be so! little did he know seeds had been planted by that church and his parents that hadn't yet sprouted their fruit.

His father took the family up north to camp, to have fun, and teach them to live off the land! Returning back home every week, his new friends tested him by teasing and antagonizing him, but quickly found out that though he was different, he wasn't weak!

After trying unsuccessfully to beat him up and bully him, they allowed him to join them in what was really an Accelerated downward spiral! he had no idea how devious the devil was at tricking people into thinking bad was good. His newfound friends began to teach him new bad habits. He learned about sarcasm-the danger of allowing anyone into your personal space to sucker punch you and to throw the first blow in a Fight and make it count. How to Sell and Do Drugs. His father noticed him hanging out with his friends, one day, he warned him, saying, "Son, you are envying the fact that those kids are out into the late-night hours of the night. but they are out late because their parents don't love them, and they probably don't make it into their 20s, and if you continue, neither will you!"

"Ok," he told his dad, but secretly continued to hang with them, and even though they sold drugs and taught him to do all testable and vile acts of evil, he felt noticed, appreciated, and loved. He noticed an inappropriate magazine one day at school on the ground, and seeing those images, began a Downward spiral of not respecting women as women but as objects to receiving pleasure! Lusting after them, he met a Woman and lost his virginity. Later, he found out she had gotten pregnant. He was super excited about being a new father but tragically lost his unborn child to a Miscarriage because the woman didn't want to keep the child. He felt his pain was deeper than an ocean, but it had only just begun. At 17 years old, he was already asking big questions: Why am I still here? What Purpose Does God Have for Me?

And because they hardened their hearts against me, I will stretch out my hand. Ephraim's Glory Shall Fly Away Like a Bird-No Birth, No Pregnancy, No Conception, I Will Love Them No More; All Their Princes Are Rebels; Even If They Bear Children, I Will Slay Their Cherished Offspring.

But he had a praying mother. He continued to attend church with his family. In his early high school years, he was on the marching band and swim team!

But after school, he foolishly thought he was living the life! From fast money one of his friends from selling drugs made enough money to buy a fancy car a month later he was that friend's pallbearer!

When you are eating hate, you are always empty, and it shows! He saw people get slaughtered. People's grandmothers assaulted, throwing up gang signs. Dare you to do something about it! And this was life. He dated a few women, not knowing the proper way to treat a woman none of the relationships had longevity, and every girlfriend that got pregnant, miscarried.

Ephraim Is Smitten, Their Root Is Dried Up, They Shall Bear No Fruit: Their Glory Yea Though They Bring Forth, Yet Will I Slay the Fruit of Their Womb? Their glory shall fly away like a Bird There shall be no birth, none with a child, and no conception!

Fast Forward: He met another woman and stayed with her for three years, and they decided they wanted to get married, but she later found out that she was going to have to do a prison bid from a long time ago for crimes committed in her past and tragically committed suicide. He felt like everything he touched, died. He felt like dying inside, and nobody knew it but him. It was almost like he was wrapped in a dark fog that darted in and out of his life and seemed to grip him and paralyze him; he didn't know it was depression. But he had a praying mother. After high school, he got a job and was in the streets the rest of the time. The devil tricked him into speaking bitterly to his father and turning his back on his family.

Oh, the Words Once Said in Life That You Can't Take Back: He ate as few meals as he could and still survived. The streets taught him no emotions from a king, seeing if anyone noticed or cared. He also decided that, since he had the choice, he wouldn't go to church. He didn't care anymore, and he didn't think God would want him. Fast forward a few years. He met another woman, got away from the streets for about 2 years, and was working full-time at a good job. Things started looking up again.

One day after work, he got into a bitter verbal argument with this woman, because she wanted to go out for something that was important to her. Being too tired to even think about it at that moment, nasty words were spoken to each other, and he stormed out of the house. He got some liquor and went back to the streets that night. He and his friends were involved in a shootout with one of the biggest gangs in the city!

He was shot seven times that night. As he lay there bleeding out, he cried out to God in distress, He said Not Like This God, But Little did he know that an evangelist had told his father two days earlier to go home and anoint the doors and windows of his home because his youngest son would be fighting for his life and His father had done so and prayed in advance.

I am poured out like water, and all my bones are out of joint! my heart is like wax; it has melted within. Dogs have encompassed me; a company of evildoers has enclosed me; they have pierced my hands and feet. and now my life ebbs away. Days of suffering have all gripped me. Night pierces my bones. My gnawing pains never rest. In his great power, God becomes like clothing to me. he binds me like the neck of my garment.

The doctors told him that out of 15 people with the same gunshot wounds, he was the only one who survived. A bullet missed his heart by 3 inches and came out under his left arm. They wanted to amputate his right leg because of the swelling in his thigh but a surgeon who was on his way out of town received a phone call and decided to cancel his trip. Upon the renowned surgeon decision, they did not amputate his leg, the large-size caliper bullet remained in his main artery in that leg! He lost a pint and a half of blood before he even arrived at the hospital, he did not know GOD Had his hand on him the entire time. When he woke from the coma the first thing he did was check to see if his manhood remained and seeing that he still had it he said out Loud, "He wasn't ready to give up everything and was negotiating with God in the beginning, saying, 'Lord, if you let me live, I will give up masturbation. He wasn't ready to submit every area to God fully yet. Doctor told him that he would never walk again but he taught himself to walk again, and he was using his hatred to get strong again for revenge on those involved but God had other Plans. Even that did not make him change. Still, he hardened his heart toward GOD, and now plunged into a world of taking prescription drugs. As he taught himself how to walk again, he started off taking them as prescribed then after getting cut off of them cold turkey! Because of his disobedience, God turned him over to his own devices and he went from selling drugs to doing some of the very drugs he had been poisoning others with! But my people would not listen to me; Israel would not submit to me. So, I gave them over to their stubborn hearts, to follow their own devices. If my people would only listen to me, if Israel would only follow my ways, how quickly i would subdue their enemies and, turn my hand against their foes! Those who hate the lord would cringe before him, and their punishment would last forever. But you would be fed with, the finest of wheat; with honey, from the rock, I would satisfy you:

He turned to hardcore drugs such as heroin, fentanyl, crack cocaine, methamphetamines, and anything you could get his hands on. He did not care, and he didn't care if his friends knew that he was doing it! During that time, he saw friends die right and left. Becoming a full-fledged addict, doing every kind of drug, and now even using needles himself. He witnessed people become the very things they hated, Good

Women became prostitutes, loving parents cheated on each other and left their kids to the protection of strangers to be abused, and molested. People would intentionally give others dirty needles to infect them because they were infected!

Strong men turned to homosexuality! People would jump him, hit him, and betray him over disputes and drugs that had he been sober. He would have been destroyed single-handedly. He would adapt and be whoever he needed to be to get the drugs he was on at the time. At some points, he spent weeks sometimes months living in abandoned houses with drugs being his only food and water. His pride wouldn't let him reach out for help from his family because his heart was cold, he would see people OD as others watched and sometimes people continued getting high as if nothing happened! He would even sometimes bring them back from OD by smacking them or putting cold ice under their armpit or CPR or Narcan and shaking them until life returned to them and then he would go right back to getting high! When people would OD off drugs, he and other addicts wanted to get that same batch, they had used because it was strong! He literally did not care if he lived or died! And this cycle continued for years!

Fast forward a few more years. He continued a life of crime and stayed distant from his family, but 1 day, on one of his many arrests, and went to jail, GOD took the scales off his eyes and everything suddenly felt different. He Saw things for what they actually were as he realized; that the streets had an expiration date on them, and he wanted out!

So, for the first time in his life, he went into his cell and completely surrendered to God, his life, his soul, everything, and made a covenant. He told God, wherever you want me to go and wherever you lead, I will follow, and for the first time, he felt a peace come over him like God was saying, "Ahhhhh I heard you were looking for me. BUT WHERE

THERE WERE 2 SETS OF FOOTPRINTS, I WALKED ALONGSIDE YOU, AND WHEN THERE WAS ONE SET OF FOOTPRINTS, I CARRIED YOU!!!"

He had no idea what God had in store for him, but he rested in faith. Little did he know that even though he had been struggling with the challenges that life had to throw at him, His family had been quietly praying and planning on his behalf to put him in a program. He called his brother from jail and found out that, upon his consent, he would be transported to the program. Upon arrival, he firmly stated that there was no way I was going in there and said, Lord, if you want me to stay, send me a sign. He heard nothing, but instead, he remembered his covenant with God and stayed. Three days later, the Lord sent a sign in the form of a new roommate, Brett, which in Hebrew means Covenant! And he remembered the Covenant he had made with God in Jail. Through maintenance, godly counselors, and strenuousness sessions and classes, the hard work paid off, and he began to discover his root problems and that there were much worse addictions than what he had gone through, like selling drugs and getting high, like Pride, Lust, and Anger, and that they stemmed from grief and P.T.S.D.

God said, this third I will put into the fire. I will refine them like silver and test them like gold. They will call on my name, and I will answer them. I will say they are my people, and they will say the Lord is our God the crazy part is the whole time I was living in addiction and I was trying to fix myself and I didn't realize the very meaning of my name was the key to me getting free because in Hebrew the name Joshua means GOD IS SALVATION!

There is no doubt I will stumble along the way. But, as this new season in my life takes shape, I am not afraid God has charged me with pulling someone else up out of the mud and being a light to others. I embrace these challenges and am excited to see what the future holds now that my footing is firm! Our Lord Jesus had his hands pierced with nails-all the times that our hands have hurt people and done cruel and nasty things that we shouldn't have! He also had his feet pierced, and nails were driven through them. For all the times that our feet have walked places we know we should not have been and stayed there, even though our conscience was telling us to get out! And Yeshua had his brow pierced with a crown of thorns.

For all the times that our minds have thought evil thoughts or shameful things! There, the Son of God hung on the cross to rescue us, and we still act as though we are not free because we hold ourselves in bondage when Yeshua already did the work! JESUS Is the Word. The Word Was Put to Death. The Word Was Pierced. The Word Dripped Blood. The Word Was Maimed. The Word Was Hung. The Word Is What endured The Passion. The Word Was Nailed. The Word Is What Died. Therefore, Your Reasoning Should Begin with The Word, then and Only Then Will You Begin to Perceive the Lord! And LAST, The Man and THE Suffering He Had to Endure! The Lord Jesus Put Every Single Detail into Symbolic Language as a Gift to Be Given to Mankind So That Their Hearts Might Be Transformed Because Of It and as a Result Receive Deliverance!

Now my goal is to teach others who are broken and struggling how to get free from self-inflicted bondage and how to stay free! I definitely will use some of the money to get established and pay off some debts so I can be free to travel wherever I'm needed for this journey of bringing deliverance to the lost and forgotten and the Hopeless!

I want to be able to help others and start a non-profit organization to help the broken and forgotten. There are a lot of organizations out there that are supposed to help others, but the people who are put in power to do so lack empathy and the proper skills to do so, or they don't care. So, the person they are supposed to help goes right back out on the street. It's time for a change, which I represent because people use drugs to mask pain, and as a result, it's like putting a band-aid on a wound; it will not heal, but truth can heal!

I'm looking for people who don't care that no one helped them or wasn't there for them; they are ready to escape the generational curse by letting God be God and letting God help them to be able to help others! If this is you, reach out to me! If God puts it on your heart to bless this vision, then, in Jesus' name, it is so, and it shall be so! I would like to get started as soon as possible because every day that I wake up, I realize that a lot of other people didn't, and the sad reality is that they either died in their addiction or they died in their sin!

If you know someone else who has been able to reach them, let me know. I know that with God's Spirit in me and God on my side, I can reach them. If he wants it to be so! I want to visit rehabs, hospitals, and prisons; wherever God sends me, I shall go without hesitation! I have seen drugs make people become who they hate most. Women with morals and values turn to prostitution, loving husbands become abusive and spiteful to their wives! Good decent people turning to evil that you cannot imagine! The first step is to realize that you trying to fix yourself will not work

Give it to God and not just some of it, give it all to him the pain the brokenness the anger the unforgiveness because before GOD can begin to help or heal you, he has to be able to affect your heart first!

But with God's help, all things are possible he snatched me out of the mud of addiction and brought Life and Light to my darkness. To all who are reading this, I speak life into your situation, and I decree that you will rise up and take charge of your life! You will succeed and not fail! You will stay in your right mind and not have scattered thoughts because you matter! You will begin to walk in a purpose-driven life, and you will not get weary of your well-being in Jesus's name, and it is so it shall be so! Our ABBA Father GOD has granted humanity two paths: one of goodness and the other of evil. Within our hearts, there exist two dispositions that choose between these paths. This Is GOOD And EVIL... Now when the soul follows the good way, the souls' deeds are righteous, and sins are immediately repented. However, if the mind leans toward evil, wickedness prevails, and the evil one gains mastery, Then Even seemingly good actions can lead to evil outcomes when tainted by an evil disposition.

Consider those who lack mercy for those who serve them in evil deeds. Such duality is wickedness concealed. Likewise, someone who commits adultery while fasting or performs good deeds but ravages others through wealth remains two-faced. However, those who cling solely to goodness destroy the devil through their actions.

Remember, being single-mindedly good, even if perceived as sinful by others, is righteousness before God. So let us begin to flee from evil tendencies, imitating the Lord, and live by what is truly clean....

Be careful not be led astray by the spirit of hatred because it is more evil than any human deed. Regardless of what anyone does, a person who hates is corrupted. Those who fear the Lord and hope for good things will avoid hatred. The true hater has no love for anyone; they disparage truth, envy the successful, relish slander, and love arrogance because hatred blinds their soul.

Beware of those who hate, as it leads to lawlessness and rebellion against the Lord. Hatred rejects GODS commands about loving our neighbors and sins against God. If a brother makes a mistake, people under the spell of the spirit of hatred quickly spreads the news, eager to see him condemned and punished. If the hater is a servant, he conspires against his master, plotting harm. Hatred collaborates with envy, becoming perpetually peevish at the prosperity of others.

While love seeks to bring the dead back to life, hatred wishes to kill the living and spares no one, even for the smallest sin. The spirit of hatred, working through human frailty, aims for the death of mankind, while the spirit of love, working by God's law, seeks mankind's salvation. Hatred is evil, consorting with lies, turning small issues into big ones, and spreading slander, conflict, violence, and greed.

I tell you this, my brothers and sisters, reading this to inform you about some of the things that keep us bound in chains and hopelessness but encourage you so that you might escape hatred and the chains of hopelessness by clinging desperately to the love of the Lord. Righteousness expels hatred, and humility kills envy. The just and humble person is ashamed to commit injustice, not out of fear of judgment, but because the Lord considers his inner thoughts. He will not denounce others, as his fear of the Most High overcomes hatred.

Repentance destroys disobedience, brings light to darkness, and guides the soul to salvation. What one has not learned from human experience, they understand through repentance. Whatever human capacity anyone transgresses by, they are also chastised by. So, love your brother, drive hatred from your heart, and love one another in deed, word, and thought.

If anyone sins against you, speak to them in peace to expel the venom of hatred. Do not harbor deceit in your heart. If anyone confesses and repents, forgive them quickly. If someone denies their guilt, do not argue, as this may lead to further sin. Do not share your secrets with outsiders, as they may become your enemies out of hatred and commit great sins against you. Even if they act treacherously, be quiet, and do not become upset; those who deny will eventually repent.

If someone prospers more than you, do not be aggrieved. Pray for their complete prosperity, for this is to your advantage. Remember that all humanity dies, eventually. Instead of being jealous, offer praise to the Lord who provides good things for all. Seek out the Lord's judgments and you will gain an inheritance.

Even if someone becomes rich through evil schemes, do not be jealous. Wait for the Lord to set things right. Those who gain through evil means and repent receive forgiveness, while the impenitent receive eternal punishment. The poor but grateful man is richer than all, as he does not love foolish temptations common to mankind.

Drive hatred away from your souls and love one another with upright hearts. Follow this recipe with all of your heart and Love GOD with all your heart, pray continuously, and you will begin to get free and stay free. Teach these principles to your children as well. Now getting back to the story about the boy. Remember that boy from the story who went to jail? Well, he died to himself in that cell, and a man emerged from that cell. And That man writes to you Now!

1. **Prayer: Structure and Strength to Contain God's Will**

- Testimony: Transformation Through Consecration

2. **Prayer: Ascending to the Hill of the Lord**

- Testimony: Rising to a Higher Spiritual Level

3. **Prayer: Declaring the Favor of God**

- Testimony: Walking in Divine Favor

4. **Prayer: Tearing Down Altars and Restoring Destiny**

- Testimony: Breaking Spiritual Bondage

5. **Prayer: Seeking Divine Understanding and Spiritual Revelation**

- Testimony: Deepening Spiritual Awareness

6. **Prayer: Breaking Curses and Embracing the Holy Spirit**

- Testimony: Experiencing Total Freedom

7. **Prayer: Conquering Fear and Tearing Down Altars**

- Testimony: Overcoming Fear and Spiritual Hindrances

8. **Prayer: Declaring Understanding, Breaking Witchcraft, and Seeking Healing**

- Testimony: Walking in God's Healing Power

9. **Prayer: Breaking Chains and Receiving God's Favor**

- Testimony: Living in Freedom and Victory

10. **Prayer: Empowerment and Anointing for I Ministry**

- Testimony: Stepping into God's Calling

11. **Prayer: Seeking Total Grace for Obedience and Healing**

- Testimony: Embracing God's Grace and Healing

12. **Prayer: Overcoming Challenges and Finding Rest in God**

- Testimony: Finding Peace and Rest in God's Presence

13. **Prayer: Declaring God's Promises and Protection**

- Testimony: Standing Firm in God's Word

14. **Prayer: Breaking Every Spirit and Declaring Victory**

- Testimony: Experiencing Breakthrough and Restoration

Prayer To This Day

God of Abraham God of Isaac, God of Jacob, who for the salvation of men has sent forth thine only begotten son, our Lord Jesus Christ, in order that he might redeem by his own blood all of us enslaved by sin and declare us to be thy sons that we may know thee the true GOD that thou existed always to eternity, GOD without end. ONE GOD, the father acknowledged in the Son and the Holy Spirit. ONE GOD the Son glorified in father and holy spirit; One GOD the Holy Spirit worshiped in father and son and acknowledged to be truly one, the father unbegotten, the son begotten, the Holy Spirit proceeding, and in thee the father and in the Holy Spirit. Thine only begotten son, our Lord Jesus Christ, in whose name thou has given us the power to heal the sick, to cure paralytics, to expel demons, and to raise the dead, for he said unto us, verily, verily, I say unto you that whatever you shall ask in my name you shall receive: I entreat then that in his name all the multitude may be saved before the morning light shines. You make the light shine up on your creation from the light of your face in order to bring the day on the Earth, and in your heavenly dwelling there is an inexhaustible light of another kind; it is an inexpressible splendor from the lights of your face! Accept my prayer and let it be sweet to you, and also the sacrifice that you yourself made through me who searched for you received me. Favorably teach me and make known to your servant what you have promised. Hear, O LORD, the prayer of your servant and give to the petition of your creature. Attend to my words as far as I shall live, and as long as I have understanding, I will answer, Oh Father, who art in heaven. Hallowed be thy name, may thy kingdom come, thy will be done in my life and on earth, Jehovah nissi, in the name of Jesus, deliver me right now from all sin, deliver my family from all sins, in the name of Jesus, every familiar spirit roaming around my life and my family's life or my destiny. I decree and declare Let the fire of the Holy Ghost rest upon me. This day, give us this day. Abba Father, give me deliverance. This day, open a door for me. This day, heal me. This day, strengthen me. This day, heal my parents. This day, fix my finances. This day, give me power to complete my assignment. This day, open a door. This day, give me a lift. This day, father. I decree and I declare a speedy manifestation of every prophetic word that is upon my life. Jehovah Nissi, you have spoken. Let it come to pass today. Father in this season, give evidence to my Christian experience, give me genuine results, even now bring me to a realm of authentic results. I'm tired of running around telling people that I am a Christian. I'm tired of telling people I love you without proof. I'm tired of telling people that I serve you, Elohim, without proof. 1 ¹m tired of telling people that I'm living for you without proof. Father, give evidence to my Christian experience; give evidence to my loving you; give evidence to my trust in you; give evidence to my living for you; I decree and I declare as long as I live!!! I become, by the grace of God, an agent of appropriating that which is finished in Christ that for the sake of myself and my family, who have been oppressed by spirits, that yoke begins to break even now. Everything that is not of God must let me go today, I decree, and I declare that every force that is tied down my destiny must let me go now... in the name of Jesus myself and my family played by every curse, curse of untimely death, curse of failure. At the edge of breakthrough, I decree, and I declare as I shout Jesus, those altars must break and give way now. 123 be released 1 am released. My family is released. My business is released. My health is released. My finances are released, my destiny is released, everything that concerns me is released, I decree, and I declare whatever has buried the name of my family and my destiny the name of Jesus by the fire of the Holy Ghost.

I declare May that veil be torn right now over my life and over my family's life. May that veil be torn right now. I decree and I declare whatever mysterious sicknesses that is eating up my finances or my family's finances that is eating up my energy or my vitality by the power of that race Christ from the dead. I declare that that demonic altar of authorization over my body and my finances is canceled. Now decree and I declare any areas of my life where I have failed or been forgotten by the power that raised Christ from the dead, and in the name that is above all names. I consult the greatest counselor general, and I declare by the spirit of the living God that favor will speak for me this time around. May favor speak for me. I decree, and I declare, every spirit that has brought me down, God bought me by himself so. I declare I am released, I decree, and I declare as I rise, I step into an arrangement and a level of strange testimonies in the name of Jesus Christ, and anyway, I'm trusting God for a job for me and my family, or anything that kills my spiritual life, destroys my health, causes enemies, or multiplies my sorrows is not from God; therefore, I decree between now and the end of August in the name that is above all names, and by the power of prophecy from the North East Southwest, may God give me a strange testimony. Abba Father I believe that whatever you are going to do for me is going to surprise me beyond my wildest imagination. I decree and I declare, and the name that is above all names everything that will make me laugh and celebrate between now and the next two weeks, whatever it is by all godly means, I declare it will happen for me whatever God has to do to make me laugh. For victory being established between now and the next two weeks, I declare that it will happen for me speedily. I decree and I declare, and the name above all is the oil of favor that can come up on a man's head that can come up on his hands and feet and rewrite his story. I stretch my hand, and I declare anywhere that I have been struggling with finances, ministry, and health, I began to receive the oil of favor even now. Father, I decree and I declare every curse every enchantment every demonic arrangement orchestrated by men and by spirits against my life and my destiny. Let it be destroyed now every curse and enchantment against my life against my health against my finances against my prosperity. I declare by the blood of the eternal covenant be broken. In the name of Jesus, and it is so!

PRAYER TESTIMONY# 1

Testimony:

There was a time in my life when everything seemed to be falling apart. Every effort I made was met with resistance, and the weight of shame and failure was overwhelming. I felt trapped in a cycle of defeat and despair. It was during this time that I discovered the power of declaring God's promises over my life.

I began to decree and declare victory, healing, and restoration in the name of Jesus. With each declaration, I felt a shift in my spirit. The heavy burdens began to tilt, and I started to see breakthroughs in areas where I had previously faced only obstacles. My health improved, relationships were restored, and opportunities that had once seemed out of reach became attainable.

One of the most profound changes was the transformation in my mindset. I moved from a place of doubt and defeat to one of faith and expectancy. I witnessed firsthand the power of speaking life into my circumstances and aligning my words with God's promises.

Today, I can confidently say that the Lord has raised me from the dust of shame and decorated my life with His favor and blessings. This prayer has been a cornerstone in my journey toward freedom and victory, and I am forever grateful for the power of faith-filled declarations.

DECREE AND DECLARE PRAYER

In the name of Yeshua, I decree and I declare Abba Father that you kill anything that is troubling me or my family or my parents, this night all unclean spirits lose me and my family. In the name of Yeshua any beings planted in myself and my family that has been planted by the enemy to destroy destiny, to destroy life, to manipulate, to cause divination, I come against you in the name of he who has the key of David. I come against you tonight in the name of Yeshua. Is it not written that every tree that my heavenly father has not planted must be rooted out tonight? I root it out I root it out in the name of Yeshua, all chains that have kept us bound are to be broken now in the name of Yeshua. All chains begin to break and give way and in Yeshua's name, I bring an end to what has harmed my family for many years. It begins to break even now. All chains begin to break even now all foundations of evil and my family and my parents and myself I come against it now in the name of YESHUA, the shadow of death that has been cast against Phyllis Oren and my family and myself I send it back to the sender in YESHUA'S name that burning in our womb I remove that fire in the name of YESHUA I bind and break the Yoke in the name of Yeshua release your captors in the name of Yeshua I decree and I declare there is a mass release in the spirit I decree and I declare No weapon formed a fashioned against us Shall prosper people will go to the shrine against me and my family and all of them will die in Yeshua's Name. I release the bondages over myself and over my family and over my parents in the name of YESHUA.

TESTIMONY # 2

Testimony:

There was a time when my family and I were under severe spiritual attacks. It seemed as though every step forward was met with two steps back. We felt bound by unseen chains, our lives manipulated by forces beyond our understanding. The constant struggle brought us to our knees, and it was during this dark period that we turned to the power of prayer with unwavering faith.

One night, I fervently prayed this prayer, calling upon the name of Yeshua to break every chain and remove every unclean spirit troubling us. As I declared each word, I felt an overwhelming sense of authority and peace. I knew that the words I spoke were being backed by divine power.

In the days that followed, we began to notice remarkable changes. Situations that seemed impossible began to turn around. Opportunities that had been blocked suddenly opened up. The oppressive heaviness that had lingered over our family was lifted, replaced by a renewed sense of hope and freedom.

We witnessed firsthand the breaking of generational curses and the uprooting of evil foundations that had plagued our lineage for years. The shadow of death and despair was cast away, and a new light dawned upon our lives.

Today, I can boldly testify that no weapon formed against us has prospered. The chains have been broken, and we walk in the liberty and blessings that Yeshua has provided. This prayer marked the beginning of a new chapter of deliverance and victory for my family, and we are eternally grateful for the power of faith and the mighty name of Yeshua.

PRAYERS FOR IMMORALITY

In the name of Yeshua, my lens has strengthened. The spirit that has been troubling me is being consumed with the fires of God. Even now I have been plagued by immoral thoughts, pornography, and spiritual wives but tonight the yoke will break, the yoke will break, the Yoke will break. In the name of Yeshua, Satan has been preventing me from reaching the Pinnacle of my calling. Tonight, I break that Yoke, Lord Jesus. I belong to you, I'm your property, please forgive me for trespassing. Forgive me, forgive me, wash me with your blood in the name of Yeshua. I belong to you so it is illegal for me to be violated spiritually so I decree and I declare and I bring an end to every spiritual union, every illegal Union. Let it end tonight, let it end tonight in the name of Yeshua, Out Loud Father. In the name of Yeshua, I come lifting myself up for being the victim of masturbation, the work of unclean spirits, the work of defiling spirits, and illegal spiritual unions that have stood against my advancement, stood against many things in my life that have constituted a basis of reproach in my destiny. Today, I break that yoke over my life in the name of Jesus, I break that yoke over my life in the name of Jesus. Let the appetite for masturbation dry up, even now, the appetite for pornography has dried up. I cast out that unplanned Spirit in The Name of Yeshua and this false Spirit of the darkness joining yourself with me to resist God tonight. I present the blood of Yeshua and I rebuke you and I bind you in the name of YESHUA anywhere in my life or when I was afflicted by altars of darkness and the spirit was taking advantage of me and has tormented me, hear me and hear my voice you spirit of darkness. I break your yoke. In the name of YESHUA ss I speak, the fires of the holy ghost are upon you. Satan RELEASE YOUR CAPTIVES in the name of Yeshua. Thank you, Lord I decree and I declare I'm going back with another fire, a fire that the devil cannot contend with fire that was a shame the enemies of the aliens to fly in YESHUA'S name and it is so it shall be so.

TESTIMONY # 3

For many years, I struggled with deep-seated issues of immorality. Thoughts and behaviors that I knew were wrong had a stronghold over me. The battle against pornography and so.

Ritual bondage was relentless, and despite my efforts, I found myself entangled in a cycle of shame and defeat.

One night, in utter desperation, I cried out to God with this prayer. I invoked the name of Yeshua and declared freedom over my life. As I prayed, I felt an intense heat, a burning sensation that I knew was the Holy Spirit working within me. The words I spoke were not just utterances; they were powerful declarations backed by divine authority.

From that moment, significant changes began to occur. The cravings and thoughts that once seemed insurmountable began to diminish. The stronghold of pornography and other immoral thoughts started to break. I experienced a newfound sense of purity and liberation that I had never known before.

The transformation was not just internal but also visible in my life. Relationships improved, my confidence grew, and my focus on my divine calling sharpened. The chains that had bound me were shattered, and I walked in a new level of freedom and holiness.

Today, I testify that the yoke of immorality has been broken. I no longer struggle with the same thoughts and behaviors that once held me captive. I am free, delivered by the power of Yeshua, and filled with a fire that the enemy cannot contend with. This prayer marked a pivotal moment in my spiritual journey, leading to a life of victory and purity. Praise be to Yeshua for His deliverance and mercy.

Prayer For Hearing And Seeing God's Signs

ABBA Father helps me to not be careless let me be able to read the signs intelligibly, there are signs coming to me because activities are taking place in the spirit. Give me the ability to be able to read the signs, I must be able to read the signs because when spirits go to work, they litter the corridor of their operation with signs that I can pick, that I can study, patterns that I can open and study. Give me the grace not to be careless, give me the ability to be able to read the signs and quicken me so that I may know what to do as a contender for Destiny, a contender for the promises of God, a contender for the intent of the Holy Spirit. I need the wisdom to be able to interpret the wisdom of the signs, to interpret the signs! there's nothing that happens in the natural suddenly. If I am alive in the spirit, I will see the signs before! When a man rises the holy spirit will give him so many signs and he will see and understand what God wants him to do. I will be given the opportunity to be able to prepare my heart for the big things that are about to take place Jehovah Nissi. I asked for wisdom I don't want to be ignorant anymore, I don't want to be daft anymore, I don't want to be a victim anymore so I pray to give me insight, give me understanding. I want to be able to read the signs around my life and know when to take my journey, know when it's time to fight, to know when it is time to resist, when is time to arise in Yeshua's Name and it is so it shall be so.

TESTIMONY# 4

Testimony:

For a long time, I struggled with understanding the signs and patterns in my life. Events would happen that caught me off guard, and I often felt like I was a step behind. This left me feeling vulnerable and unprepared for the challenges I faced. I knew that there were spiritual activities influencing my life, but I lacked the wisdom and insight to interpret them correctly.

One day, I decided to pray this prayer with all my heart. I asked the ABBA Father for the ability to read the signs and to give me the wisdom needed to understand the spiritual messages around me. As I prayed, I felt a profound sense of clarity and peace. I knew that God was listening and that He would equip me with the discernment I needed.

In the weeks that followed, I noticed a significant change. I began to see patterns and signs more clearly. Situations that once baffled me started to make sense. I could anticipate events and prepare myself accordingly. This newfound insight allowed me to navigate life with greater confidence and faith.

I realized that the Holy Spirit was indeed guiding me, showing me the signs and giving me the wisdom to interpret them. This prayer transformed my spiritual awareness and deepened my relationship with God. I no longer felt like a victim of circumstances; instead, I felt empowered and prepared for whatever came my way.

Today, I am thankful for the wisdom and understanding that God has bestowed upon me. I can read the signs and make informed decisions that align with His will. This has brought immense peace and direction to my life, and I am grateful for the divine guidance that now lights my path.

Prayer To Stay In The Will Of God

In the name of Yeshua, Father give me structure to contain your will, give me the ability to discover your kingdom Abba Father, give me the structure to contain your will Abba Father, grant me the grace to persist and to persevere, grant me the power to stay until the will of God is made, manifest, grant me the grace and power to stay in the place of Prayer when the devil comes to manipulate the world to bring about destruction. Grant me the power to retain your place the power to stay on the very hearts! When the kingdom of the devil comes to manipulate everything around me, grant me the grace to stay in prayer Lord, your word says having done all that you may stand when the devil begins to roar that I may stand until the fire of the Lord comes down from heaven many times. I take off like a tornado but I do not have the power to stand, teach me to never turn until I gain mastery and power from God and learn how to stand. Oh God! give me the grace to stand against the wows of the evil one Abba Father, I live for you and I ask tonight that you make your grace available cost the least among our numbers to become as strong as David because a little one will become a thousand, a small one will become a nation, though your beginning is small, your little hand shall be greatly increased In Yeshua's Name. I decree and I declare I begin to rise up in my spirit, even now I rise up in my spirit In Yeshua's name. I cast away all Idols and I destroy that high place dedicated to the queen of heaven, Jehovah Nissi. I ask that any areas of my Life or anyone around me that I require strength to overcome anything not of you so that I can take a stand for you wherever I am to where I can say 'ok' enough. I take my journey in the spirit now and I will journey until I find you Elohim. I ask that tonight you stretch forth your hand and administer strength to my spirit. Is it not written that you will strengthen us with might by your spirit in the inner man ABBA Father, any altars that have held me or my family in chains let there be Fire on that Altar, let there be Fire on that Altar. I release Fire on that Altar, Come Out!!!!! In Yeshua's name, all blinding spirits plaguing me be arrested, let blinding yokes be removed in the Yeshua's Name. I speak to my eyes see In Yeshua's Name and it is so it shall be so.

TESTIMONY# 5

Testimony:

I have often struggled with maintaining the structure and strength necessary to live out God's will for my life. There were times when I would feel a surge of inspiration, only to lose momentum and fall back into old patterns. The inconsistency made it difficult for me to progress spiritually and left me vulnerable to the enemy's schemes.

One evening, I decided to pray earnestly for structure and strength. I called upon Abba Father, asking for the grace to persist and the power to stand firm in the face of adversity. As I prayed, I felt a deep conviction and a surge of strength within my spirit. It was as if a fire had been ignited inside me, empowering me to overcome the spiritual battles that lay ahead.

In the days that followed, I began to notice a transformation. I was more disciplined in my spiritual practices and more attuned to the signs and movements of the Spirit. Situations that previously overwhelmed me no longer had the same power. I found myself standing firm, equipped with the grace and strength I had prayed for.

The idols and high places that once held sway over my life were dismantled. I was able to say "enough" and take my spiritual journey seriously, seeking and finding God in deeper ways. The altars that had held my family in chains were consumed by divine fire, breaking the bonds and bringing freedom.

This prayer brought a profound change in my life. I now have the structure to contain God's will and the strength to stand against the wiles of the evil one. My spiritual eyes are open, and I see clearly the path that God has set before me. This journey has brought me closer to Elohim, and I am grateful for the empowerment that has come through fervent prayer.

Praise be to Yeshua for the strength and structure He has provided. I am rising up in my spirit, living in victory, and walking in the fullness of God's promises. This testimony is a testament to the power of prayer and the faithfulness of our heavenly Father.

Prayer To Ascend God's Holy Hill

In the name of Yeshua, this night, I ascend, I ascend, I ascend, I know that it's a holy place and that it would demand consecration of me. I know that it will demand righteous living from me. I am willing to ascend to the hill of the Lord your word says who shall ascend until the hill of the Lord who shall stand in his holy place, he that has clean hands, and a pure heart, and just in case I have done anything wrong I received the blood right now because I am doing business this weekend. There are territories that Satan has encroached but I decree and declare they're going to be restored back to me because I'm going to contend. I put Satan on notice, lift up your heads, lift up your heads, lift up your heads, I'm going to do some contention and that's why I am saying Abba Father I'm willing to ascend your hill, I'm willing to stand in your holy place. I decree and declare I am being trained to stand and contend for my father's estate. There are things that Yahweh has committed into my hands and he has committed them so that I can keep them beyond the reach of encroachment and God will begin to empower me and anyone under the sound of my voice with what it takes to stand, to contend, and to reclaim the territory that God has committed into my hands. I accept your invitation, I accept your invitation, I decide to ascend into your hill, I decide to come into your holy place, I embrace the values of your kingdom and I decree and I declare in Yeshua's name, my soul will not agree with the devil. There will be no agreement, there will be no compatibility, and Satan will find no ground in my life or around my life in the mighty name of Yeshua. Thank you, Lord, in the name of he, who holds the key of David so I asked the Holy Ghost to look upon me and my family and let a mighty Grace of Liberty descend upon us from on high all limitations that have stood in the way of actualizations, let all such Yokes be taken out now, in the name of Yeshua. Anywhere where I have been contending with the spirit of delay, I stand with you and face and I discomfit that enemy now and in the name of Yeshua so let it be written. Let it be done in YESHUA'S name and it is so it shall be so.

TESTIMONY # 6

Testimony:

There came a time in my life when I felt a strong pull to ascend to a higher spiritual level. I realized that this ascension would demand consecration, righteous living, and a pure heart. Understanding the significance of this call, I decided to respond wholeheartedly. I prayed fervently, asking God to cleanse me and prepare me to stand in His holy place.

I knew there were territories in my life that Satan had encroached upon. I needed to reclaim these areas and restore them under God's dominion. As I prayed, I felt an overwhelming sense of empowerment. I declared my willingness to ascend to God's hill and to contend for what was rightfully mine. I put Satan on notice, declaring that he had no place in my life.

In the days that followed, I experienced a significant shift. I felt a divine strength within me, equipping me to stand and reclaim the territories that had been taken. I began to see restoration in areas of my life that had been under siege. The values of God's kingdom became more evident in my daily walk, and my soul found no agreement with the enemy.

One of the most remarkable changes was the newfound liberty that descended upon my family and me. Limitations that had hindered our progress were broken, and the yokes that had bound us were lifted. The spirit of delay that had plagued us was defeated, and we began to see the actualization of God's promises.

This prayer marked a turning point in my spiritual journey. By ascending to the hill of the Lord, I discovered a new level of intimacy with God and a greater authority in spiritual matters. The Holy Ghost granted us the grace of liberty, empowering us to live out God's will with confidence and purpose.

Praise be to Yeshua for His faithfulness. This testimony stands as a testament to the power of consecration, prayer, and unwavering faith in God's promises. In Yeshua's name, it is so, and it shall be so.

Prayer Of Declarations To Start Your Day

I decree and declare that this is the day that the Lord has made, and I will be glad in it. I prophesied, and I declare that gentiles come to my light, Kings to the brightness of my rising in the name of Jesus Christ. I will not give birth to sorrow or anger in the name of Jesus. My mind is fruitful, the favor of the Lord is upon me in the name of Jesus. I will escape from all deceitful things that come my way. In the name of JESUS, turn me into an influence for the sake of your glory. For the sake of your glory, not to build an empire for myself. Just so that as men look at me, I can point them to Jesus. As they look at my life, I can point them to Jesus Jehovah Nissi. Give me influence by the spirit of God manifest unto me, grace over systems manifest unto me, Grace over structures manifest unto me, Grace over the hearts of men in the name of Jesus. I receive that Grace, Lord. My life will never make substantial progress until the favor of God is upon my head. Look upon me with favor this year, look up on my family with your favor upon my head, favor upon on my hands, favor upon my destiny, favor upon my life, favor upon my ministry, favor with God favor, with men a sign and a Wonder the favor of God in the name of Jesus. Release upon me, Oh God, that Grace. Release upon me, oh God that Grace, that speaks to the clouds. Release upon us the grace that sends the lightning and they say, "Here we are at your beck and call." The grace to call, animate objects, inanimate objects, to come into my space in the name of Jesus. Lord, in advance I surrender my achievements in advance. I surrender my exploits in advance. I surrender the name, the fame, the increase it is for Your Glory and it remains for Your Glory as I glorify your son your son will glorify me. Lord, as I increase in ministry, I vow that you'll be glorified as I increase in business. I vow that the Nations will know you as a doer as you multiply your grace, your wisdom, and your power in me. Lord, I am here as a Sower. Grant me the grace to receive precious seeds and to sew it with wisdom that I was sow to the spirit so that I Will of the spirit reap life everlasting the grace to participate in every aspect of the service remaining in prayer, in listening, and in receiving by faith. I receive seed now; I receive seed now in JESUS' Name and it is so shall it be.

TESTIMONY# 7

Testimony:

I have always believed in the power of declaring God's favor over my life, but it was during a particularly challenging season that I truly experienced its transformative power. I found myself in a situation where progress seemed impossible, and my efforts felt fruitless. I knew I needed divine intervention and favor to overcome these obstacles.

One morning, I decided to decree and declare this prayer over my life. I spoke with conviction, believing that God's favor would change my circumstances. As I declared that gentiles would come to my light and kings to the brightness of my rising, I felt a shift in my spirit. I asked Jehovah Nissi for influence and grace over systems, structures, and the hearts of men, committing my success to His glory.

Almost immediately, doors that had been closed began to open. Opportunities that I had not even sought out came to me. My mind became more fruitful, and I escaped deceitful situations that had previously ensnared me. People began to notice the change in my life, and I was able to point them to Jesus, attributing all success to His glory.

One of the most profound changes was the favor that God placed upon my head, hands, destiny, life, and ministry. The grace that I had prayed for manifested in tangible ways.

Financial breakthroughs, personal growth, and spiritual depth all came into my life. The influence I had prayed for materialized, not for my glory, but so that others could see Christ through me.

As I surrendered my achievements and exploits to God, I witnessed His power in ways I had never imagined. The more I committed to glorifying Him, the more He elevated me. This prayer became a cornerstone of my faith journey, reminding me that true success comes from aligning with God's will and seeking His favor.

Today, I stand as a testament to the power of declaring God's favor. My life is a reflection of His grace and glory, and I continue to sow seeds with wisdom, reaping everlasting life by the Spirit. This testimony is a powerful reminder that when we seek God's favor and commit our ways to Him, He will indeed make our paths straight and our lives a beacon of His goodness.

PRAYER FOR DELIVERANCE

Oh God! Arise, oh God, that rides upon the winds. Arise over my spirit, over my family, over my mind, over my will, in Jesus' name. I tear down altars plaguing me. I use prayer as a system of authorization. This curse must stop this limitation, must cease this yoke, that is keeping me stagnant must be broken in JESUS' Name. This bad luck in my life must stop in the name of Jesus. In the name of Jesus tonight, I stand on behalf of myself and my family and I decree and declare that every altar that is speaking against my destiny, I tear it down tonight. Altars of delay, altars of blindness, altars of failure, altars of stagnation, I tear it down in the name of Jesus. Every legal access I have given for these altars to speak against me knowingly and unknowingly, tonight I invoke the blood. Let the blood speak every legal access I have given any Altar of darkness. I am delivered now and even the lawful captives shall be delivered in the name of Jesus. Altars of poverty, altars of delay, altars of failure in my life, I speak to you in the name of he, who has the key of David. I tear you down and release my destiny. Now altars of stagnation, I speak against you, I curse you, I destroy your efforts by the god of Heaven. In the name of Jesus, altars that are associated with territories fighting my destiny because of where I'm coming from. I prophesy tonight and I decree and declare your hold is broken over my Life. I come against you now, in Jesus' name. Every delayed blessing that should have happened in my life and was delayed because of these altars tonight by prophecy, I call you back to my life, restore relationships, restore destiny, restore my assignment, restore everything dead in my life, restore my purpose, restore my mind, restore my finances, restore my ministry in the name of (Say the Names of Who You Are Praying For). I stand as an Altar and I bring you out of this dungeon. I bring you out of this wasteful living. I decree and declare that the Altar fighting you is broken in the name of Jesus. I speak to the East, I speak to the West, I speak to the North, I speak to the South, everywhere my favor is in the name of Jesus. I command it to my life now. Lord, I'm part of an apostolic family, the Altar you have erected must stand for me. I want my life to show it from today forward. Yahweh, I invoke the altar that you have with your servant in the name of Jesus. I decree and declare that the spirit of Prayer and supplication is the grace to pray. I receive it right now, fresh fire on my altar, fresh Grace to fast fresh Grace, intercede fresh Grace for warfare, I command everyday prayer life around my life to come back to life in the name of Jesus Holy Spirit. I ask that you manifest yourself once again in my life Holy Spirit. I cry for intimacy with you Spirit of the Living God. Do not be far from me again, let it not be that I'm just a stranger. We saw closer than this and something happened in Jesus' name. Jehovah Nissi restore my intimacy with you, restore my fellowship that I once had with you in the name of the that is above all names. I command those altars to be broken now. I judge those altars now by fire. Total Deliverance comes down in the name of Jesus. Any 1 of my sisters whose family and Destiny are under siege anywhere in my life or my sister's life where they have made a covenant with the enemy. Anyone who passed through fire to make a covenant with my destiny, or their destiny in the name that is above all names. I decree and declare upon being free now in the name of Jesus from those Yokes that cause fibroids, those Yokes that cause lumps around your body. I curse it by the God of heaven in the name of Jesus. I break that spiritual marriage in the name of Jesus, I command judgment on any strange spirit in the name of Jesus. A place where the word of God let that sword of Deliverance work for me now, I command that double-edged sword to locate everyone including myself who is in need of total Deliverance. I command it no escape in Jesus' name, every Mark of disfavor that is upon my life or my family's life where man should bless me but something about Me causes irritation, I command that Mark be erased from my life now in Jesus' name I decree and declare that the demon sitting on my financial Glory on my family's financial Glory. I clean it out of the way right now in the name of JESUS Christ and it is so.

TESTIMONY # 8

Testimony:

For a long time, my family and I struggled under the weight of spiritual battles that we couldn't understand. We faced delays, stagnation, and financial hardships that seemed insurmountable. It felt as though there were altars speaking against our destiny, holding us back from the blessings and progress we knew were meant for us.

One night, in desperation, I prayed this prayer with fervent faith. I called upon God to rise and intervene in our lives, to tear down every altar that was speaking against us. As I declared the words, I felt a powerful shift in the atmosphere. The prayer was not just words; it was a divine mandate breaking chains and demolishing strongholds.

In the weeks that followed, we began to see significant changes. Long-delayed blessings started to manifest. Relationships were restored, and opportunities that had been blocked were suddenly available. Financial breakthroughs occurred, and the heavy burdens we had carried were lifted.

The most profound transformation was in our spiritual lives. The Holy Spirit renewed our intimacy with God, and we felt a deep connection that had been missing. Our prayer lives were revitalized, and we experienced fresh fire and grace for intercession and warfare.

This prayer brought total deliverance and restoration. The altars that had once spoken against us were silenced, and the curses were broken. Our lives were marked by favor and blessings, and the spirit of disfavor was erased.

Today, I testify to the power of this prayer and the faithfulness of God. He has restored our destiny, our purpose, and our financial glory. We stand as living witnesses to His mighty deliverance and unfailing love. In Jesus' name, it is so, and it shall be so.

Prayer To Change Spiritual Smell

ABBA Father, I ask you to take more of me and give me more of you in YESHUA'S name. Any smell that I have or my family has of reproach in the realm of the spirit, tonight I come to wage war against the speaking of altars. So that the Lord will arise and begin to blot out every tongue that is speaking over my life in the name of Yeshua. I speak Psalms 1:3 over my life Jehovah Nissi. Your word says: 111 "Moab hath been at ease from his youth, and he hath settled on his lees, and hath not been emptied from vessel to vessel, neither hath he gone into captivity: therefore, his taste remained in him, and his scent is not changed". So, in the name of YESHUA, if God needs to allow me to suffer a little so that my scent can change, may he do it in the name of Yeshua. If I remain in the Lee's, if I remain in my comfort zone, my scent can never change and it is God's intention to change my scent so Anna's father, change my scent today in the name of Yeshua.

Testimony # 9

Testimony:

There was a time in my life when I felt a deep sense of reproach. It seemed as though a lingering scent of failure and disappointment clung to me, affecting my relationships and opportunities. I realized that this was not just a physical issue but a spiritual one. There were altars speaking against me, keeping me in a state of stagnation and comfort that prevented growth.

One night, in desperation, I prayed this prayer with all my heart. I asked ABBA Father to take more of me and give me more of Him. I waged war against the altars and their voices, invoking the power of Yeshua's name. I spoke Psalms 1:3 over my life, declaring that I would be like a tree planted by the rivers of water, bringing forth fruit in my season. I also referenced Jeremiah 48:11, understanding that sometimes, a little suffering is necessary for transformation.

In the days that followed, I felt a profound change. God began to strip away my comfort zones, allowing me to face challenges that refined me. These experiences, though difficult. changed my spiritual scent. I noticed a shift in how people responded to me. Opportunities began to open up, and I no longer felt the weight of reproach hanging over me.

God's intention to change my scent was evident. He allowed certain trials to come my way, not to harm me, but to refine me. Through these experiences, my character and faith were strengthened. The scent of reproach was replaced with the fragrance of grace and favor.

Today, I stand as a testament to the transformative power of God. My life no longer bears the scent of reproach. Instead, it carries the sweet aroma of His presence and favor. I am grateful for the refining process and for the new scent that signifies growth, strength, and God's unending grace. In Yeshua's name, it is so, and it shall be so.

PRAYER TO EXALT MY HORN

ABBA Father, I ask that you take more of me and give me more of you. I ask, did you take more of me? Give me more of you. I decree and declare in Yeshua's name; my horn shall be exalted. Lord, you have given me the power to cast out devils, so I trust you for a stronger ministry against the kingdom of darkness in Yeshua's name. Jehovah Nissi, make me more potent, make me stronger, make me more powerful. Let something fresh begin with me, Lord. Grace me with another dimension of the operation of God - intercessions, deliverances of territories. Grace me with the authority to expel demons beyond the high side. Let the grace of God be renewed in my vessel now, in Yeshua's name. A new season comes now. The new season comes now. Your voice will be heard, Lord. I decree and declare that no power in hell can stop me or hold me down. Like a storm, the hand of God will reach forth. Whatever weapon formed or fashioned against me will not prosper! Put a deposit on my life that will make it impossible for men to ignore me. Make it impossible for men to call me non-essential. I need you to do something for me, Father. Let there be a response from heaven. Let there be a deposit in my life. Just like a businessman needs capital, the capital of the minister is the anointing, Lord. Let it be with these deposits that I do business, where I can sell Jesus. Viable marketing with the instrument of the Anointing, so the attention of my generation can be drawn back to God, in Yeshua's name. I am not non-essential. I am in the very heart of this stage. ABBA Father, you are the God of life. You are the only one who has the authority to speak, and no one can say unto you, "What doeth thou?" I'm a child of light. I am a man that has a place for favor with God, sufficient to move his hand. Lord, make me a man of sufficient stature, a man that could change the tide, a man that can manipulate the possibilities. May that mantle fall on me now, in Yeshua's name. And it is so, shall it be.

TESTIMONY# 10

Testimony:

There was a season in my life when I felt a deep yearning for more of God's presence and power. I knew that to fulfill the calling on my life, I needed a fresh anointing and a new level of grace. I prayed fervently, asking ABBA Father to take more of me and give me more of Him. I sought to be empowered and equipped to cast out devils and to stand strong against the kingdom of darkness.

As I prayed this prayer, I felt a profound shift in my spirit. The Lord began to work in me, increasing my potency and strength. I sensed a new dimension of God's operation in my life—intercessions and deliverances that went beyond anything I had experienced before. The grace of God was renewed in my vessel, and I entered a new season.

Opportunities for ministry began to open up, and I found myself equipped with the authority to expel demons and to reclaim territories for God. I declared that no power in hell could stop me, and I witnessed the truth of that declaration as the hand of God reached forth in my life. Weapons formed against me did not prosper, and the favor of God made it impossible for people to ignore the work He was doing through me.

One of the most significant changes was the deposit of God's anointing in my life. This anointing became my capital, enabling me to do the business of the Kingdom effectively. I was able to market Jesus in a way that drew the attention of my generation back to God. The anointing made me essential, positioning me at the heart of God's stage.

God's favor rested upon me, and I became a man of sufficient stature to change the tide. The mantle of influence and power fell upon me, and I began to manipulate the possibilities, bringing about God's will on earth as it is in heaven. This prayer marked a pivotal moment in my spiritual journey, transforming me into a vessel of honor and power for God's glory.

Today, I testify to the incredible work of God in my life. The fresh anointing and the new grace have empowered me to fulfill my calling and to stand firm against the forces of darkness. I am grateful for the deposit of God's anointing and for the favor that moves His hand. In Yeshua's name, it is so, and it shall be so.

Prayer To Keep Lamp Burning

In the name of Yeshua, I decree and I declare that my lamp will not go out. If my inner lamp is at work, God can make me overcome anything. Therefore, my security lies in the work of Christ within me. There is no situation that I face where I can be disadvantaged. If I am meant to work within the situation, I cannot be disadvantaged because I can do all things through Christ who strengthens me. Instead of focusing on my weaknesses and shortcomings, I will discover what Grace can do and experience it in Yeshua's name. Your word says, "And I will pour upon the house of David, and upon the inhabitants of Jerusalem, the spirit of grace and supplication; and they shall look unto me whom they have pierced; and they shall mourn for him, as one mourned for his only son, and shall be in bitterness for him, as one that is in bitterness for his first-born" (Zechariah 12:10). So, I decree and declare that no circumstance in my life can make me feel incompetent because my competence comes from understanding God's commitment to my life. I decree and declare that the spirit of Grace and supplication comes upon my life now in Yeshua's name.

TESTIMONY# 11

Testimony:

There were times in my life when I felt overwhelmed by the challenges and situations I faced. My weaknesses and shortcomings often made me feel incompetent and disadvantaged. I realized that I needed to rely not on my own strength, but on the grace and power of Christ within me.

One day, I prayed this prayer with a heart full of faith, declaring that my lamp would not go out because of the work of Christ within me. I acknowledged that my security lies in His work in me and that through Him, I could overcome any situation. As I declared this, I felt a profound sense of peace and assurance that God was indeed my strength.

In the days that followed, I experienced a remarkable transformation. Situations that previously seemed insurmountable became opportunities for God's grace to manifest in my life. I found myself able to navigate challenges with a newfound competence and confidence, knowing that my strength came from Christ.

One of the most significant changes was the outpouring of the spirit of grace and supplication upon my life. By prayer, life was revitalized, and I felt a deeper connection with God. This spirit of grace enabled me to approach life's circumstances with a sense of victory and assurance, knowing that God's commitment to me was unwavering.

No longer did I feel incompetent or disadvantaged. Instead, I walked with the understanding that God's grace was sufficient for me, and His power was made perfect in my weakness. The spirit of grace and supplication became a cornerstone of my spiritual life, empowering me to live out my faith boldly and effectively.

Today, I testify to the power of declaring God's promises over my life. The spirit of grace and supplication has transformed me, and I continue to experience the fullness of God's grace in every aspect of my life. In Yeshua's name, it is so, and it shall be so.

Prayer To Speak Life Over Yourself

Lord your word says, "Put me in remembrance let us plead together declare thou, that thou mayest be justified." That tells me that your hand is able to save, your hand is able to lift, but you are waiting on me to declare! So, in the name of Yeshua, I decree and declare. Yea, as I walk through the valley of the shadow of death, I fear no evil, for thou art with me. Thy rod and thy staff, they comfort me. Jehovah Nissi, you prepare a table for me in the presence of my enemies, anointing my hair with fresh oil. My cup runs over. I have no covenant with death. In the name of YESHUA, I decree and declare, as for me and my house, we will serve YAHWEH. Peace, be still. I decree and declare, that the Lord is my light and my salvation. Lord, you set before me life and death. I choose life, I choose victory, I choose health by the spirit of the Living God. Thousand may fall by my side, 10,000 by my right side, but none shall harm me. With my eyes, I will see the reward of the wicked. But no weapon formed against me shall prosper. I arise and shine because my light has come because the glory of the Lord has risen upon me. Gentiles come to my light, kings to the brightness of my rising. To my shame, I receive double. Where I have been deserted, I receive eternal Excellency, a joy of many generations. ABBA Father, your word says, "Let the redeemed of the Lord say so, whom he hath redeemed from the hand of the enemy." So, I declare that I have been redeemed. I won't be silent as long as I am breathing. I will always worship you Jehovah Jireh. I decree and I declare victory. My finances are not scattered, my health is fine, and I am not lazy, and I am hard working. Lord! There is an evil force, trying to discredit God in my life. I attack you in the name of he, who holds the key of David and I decree and I declare, I've made up my mind. God gave me this mouth not only to eat but to create my destiny, and I insist on it for my life, my destiny, my family, and my ministry. We rise now, we rise now. I take authority over my life, over my destiny, by the power of the Holy Ghost in Yeshua's name. For as long as I live, I will never stop praying. For as long as God is anointing me, I will never stop praying. For as long as I live, I will never ignore the word of God. Jehovah Nissi, I found your word and I ate it, and it brought joy, rejoicing, and replenishment to my soul. Heaven and Earth will pass away, but the word of the Lord will abide forever. YESHUA, disciple me and teach me to abide in you. Lord, there is a spirit attacking my influence, and a spirit taking my finances. Lord, there is a spirit attacking my passion for you. I didn't used to be like this. What happened to my prayer fire? What happened to my word fire? Something is wrong with my spiritual life. I reject depression. I release things I have no control over. I release anxiety. I release anger. I reject sickness. I reject failure. Lord, if I am to die, let me die believing in you. Touch not me or anyone around me or my family. Lord, your word says if any man is afflicted, let him pray. I've made up my mind that everybody under my roof must serve God in Yeshua's name. And it is so, it shall be so!

TESTIMONY# 12

Testimony:

There was a period in my life when I felt overwhelmed by the challenges and spiritual battles that seemed to consume me. I knew I needed to remind myself of God's promises and declare His word over my life. One night, with a heart full of determination and faith, I prayed this prayer, declaring God's protection, provision, and victory.

As I spoke each word, I Felt a profound sense of empowerment. I reminded myself that the Lord is my light and my salvation, that no weapon formed against me would prosper, and that I had been redeemed by the hand of the Almighty. I declared that my finances were not scattered, my health was secure, and that I was gaining strength in the Spirit.

In the days that followed, I noticed significant changes. The oppressive weight of depression and anxiety lifted, and my spiritual fervor was renewed. I felt a fresh anointing and a new sense of purpose. Opportunities that had been blocked began to open, and relationships that had been strained were restored. The spirit of discrediting and failure was defeated, and I walked in the victory and favor of the Lord.

This prayer became a cornerstone of my faith journey. It reminded me that my competence and strength come from God and that His word is a powerful weapon against any force that seeks to harm me. My influence and finances were no longer under attack, and I experienced a deeper intimacy with God.

Today, I stand as a testament to the power of declaring God's promises over our lives. I continue to speak His word with boldness and confidence, knowing that He is faithful to His promises. My life is a reflection of His grace and power, and I am committed to serving Him with all my heart. In Yeshua's name, it is so, and it shall be so.

Prayer To Open Your Spiritual Eyes

Holy Spirit, open the eyes of my understanding. Cause me to see what my natural eyes cannot see, cause me to see what my feelings cannot perceive. Cause me to lay hold of that which is intangible, the substance of my reality. Oh, Holy Spirit, take me to that place where lions cannot enter, that place where fierce lions cannot pass, that place where vultures cannot see. That place, that place, that place. I decree and declare in the name of Yeshua that my citizenship is of heaven. I am only manifesting on the face of the earth as an ambassador in Yeshua's name. I decree and declare that I come from heaven, derived from heaven. This world has never seen my type before. I am a spectacle crafted by the hands of God for such a time as this. Satan cannot use my mind; Satan cannot manifest through my emotions. I was designed to be separated unto God, to be God's vessel, God's mouthpiece, God's voice on the earth. Satan has no place in my body, in my soul, and in my spirit. I decree and declare that no one has ever been like me. I am a new creation and yet no one will ever be. I was crafted with a sense of uniqueness, fearfully and wonderfully made. Oh, Yeshua, you are the one who will teach my hands to fight. You're the one who will teach my feet to walk. You are the one that will cause me to speak the words of God, teach me the ways of the king. Oh, Yeshua, I want to learn your ways. I want to know your voice. I want to be able to clearly discern it over my own voice and Satan's voice. I want to understand your whisper, for it is written that there is a spirit in man that the inspiration of the Almighty gives them understanding. I declare I want understanding about the anointing that you have placed upon my life. There is a deposit, there is an investment, spiritual capital that has been placed on my life. I want to understand it, oh Yeshua. From this day forth, I want to know your voice. There is a uniqueness that is attached to my life, there is a uniqueness that is attached to my destiny. My father and mother may not know it, but you know it. Holy Spirit, take me to the place that all unjust eyes have not seen, that the lion's world has not trotted, where the fierce lions have not passed by. Show me that place, that place where angels cannot move, that place that prophets do not understand. Show me, oh Yeshua, give me your understanding, and I will live my true life. My true existence begins when I have understanding. Give me understanding, Yahweh. Holy Spirit, take more of me, give me more of you. Take more of me, give me more of you. Take more of me, give me more of you. Take more of me, give me more of you. In the mighty name of Yeshua, and it is so, it shall be so.

TESTIMONY # 13

Testimony:

Throughout my spiritual journey, I have always yearned for a deeper understanding and revelation of God's mysteries. I left a strong pull to see beyond the natural, to perceive what my physical eyes could not, and to grasp the intangible realities of the spirit. This longing led me to pray this heartfelt prayer, asking the Holy Ghost to open the eyes of my understanding and take me to a place where only divine revelation could lead.

As I prayed, I felt an overwhelming sense of peace and clarity. It was as if a veil had been lifted, and I began to perceive the spiritual dimensions that had previously been hidden from me. The Holy Spirit started to reveal things about my life, my destiny, and the anointing that God had placed upon me. I began to understand that my true identity and purpose were rooted in my heavenly citizenship and that I was crafted uniquely by God's hands for a specific mission on earth.

The revelations I received were profound. I realized that Satan had no place in my mind, emotions, or spirit because I was designed to be God's vessel and mouthpiece. This understanding gave me a new sense of confidence and authority in my spiritual walk. I began to speak and act with a boldness that I had never known before, knowing that I was fearfully and wonderfully made for such a time as this.

One of the most significant changes was my ability to discern God's voice. The Holy Spirit taught me to distinguish between my own thoughts, the enemy's whispers, and God's gentle guidance. This clarity transformed my prayer life and my daily walk with God. I found myself walking in step with the Spirit, understanding the anointing and the spiritual capital that had been invested in me.

Today, I testify to the transformative power of seeking divine understanding. The Holy Ghost has taken me to places of revelation that I never imagined possible. My spiritual eyes are open, and I live with a heightened awareness of God's presence and purpose in my life. This journey has equipped me to be a more effective ambassador of Christ, and I am grateful for the continual unfolding of God's mysteries. In Yeshua's name, it is so, and it shall be so.

Prayer For Healing

Abba Father, I ask for Total Grace for power for my Total obedience that in all you demand for me to do make good your word I obtain Grace in Yeshua's Name. I decree and declare, by grace I obtain true faith, I am lifted by grace. I decree and declare, I am rising by grace True Faith because Faith is my action of obedience, I come before you today to heal my body, mind, and Spirit.

I decree & I declare that I am a child of God, and I have been given the power to bind every negative spiritual force that may be causing sickness, disease, or infirmity in my life and to loose every positive spiritual force that can bring healing, restoration, and wholeness to every area of my life.

I bind every Spirit of sickness, disease, and infirmity that may be causing pain and suffering in my body.

I command every negative medical report or diagnosis to be nullified.

I loose the Spirit of healing, restoration, and wholeness that can bring health and wellness to every area of my life.

I also bind every Spirit of fear, anxiety, and worry that may be causing me to doubt your healing power and to live in a state of emotional distress.

I loose the Spirit of peace, comfort, and hope that could bring emotional healing and stability to my life. I declare that the blood of Jesus covers me, and I command every negative spiritual force to flee from my body, mind, and Spirit.

I thank you, God, for your healing power, love, and mercy, and I receive every healing you have in store for me.

I also pray for those suffering from illness and disease that they, too, would experience your healing power and receive the physical, emotional, and spiritual healing they need.

In Jesus' name, & it is so.

TESTIMONY# 14

Testimony:

There was a time in my life when I was overwhelmed by physical, emotional, and spiritual afflictions. The weight of sickness, anxiety, and doubt pressed heavily on me, and I felt powerless to overcome them. In my desperation, I turned to God and prayed this prayer, seeking His grace for obedience and His healing power.

As I prayed, I felt a profound sense of peace and assurance that God was with me. I declared my faith and bound every negative spiritual force that had been causing me pain and suffering. I lost the spirit of healing, restoration, and wholeness, trusting that God's power was more than enough to heal every area of my life.

In the days that followed, I began to notice remarkable changes. The physical pain that had plagued me started to diminish. Medical reports that once brought fear and uncertainty were nullified. I experienced a renewed sense of health and wellness. The emotional distress and anxiety that had kept me in bondage were replaced with a deep sense of peace and comfort.

One of the most significant transformations was in my spiritual life. My faith was strengthened, and I understood that my true strength came from God's grace. I felt a new level of obedience and commitment to His will. The realization that I had the power to bind and lose spiritual forces in my life empowered me to walk in victory and freedom.

Today, I am a living testament to God's healing power. My body, mind, and spirit have been restored, and I continue to experience His grace and mercy daily. I no longer live in fear or doubt, but in the assurance that God's healing power is at work in my life.

I am also grateful for the opportunity to pray for others who are suffering. Knowing that they, too, can experience God's healing power fills me with hope and compassion. Qty life is a testimony to the transformative power of prayer and the unending grace of God. In Yeshua's name, it is so, and it shall be so.

PRAYER AGAINST EVIL EMBARGOS

In the mighty name of YESHUA, I decree and declare that anything that is not of God, anything that is planting an embargo on my life and my family's life, programming evil and pain, in the name of YESHUA, it must give way now! Unclean altars and Yokes, give way on my family. Finally, Spirit of the Living God, Abba Father, I return to you now. I see that you are beyond just a Pentecostal phenomenon. Spirit of the Living God, you are beyond just a prayer language. Holy Ghost, you are the gift God sends to me to ensure that my life becomes and remains victorious. If Jesus needed the Holy Spirit as the Son of God, I know that me and my family also need the Holy Spirit. Ebenezer, the helper of men, your word says that Uziah prospered because he was mightily helped. So, help me, ABBA Father. I decree and declare that today is the day I am receiving my portion in the name of YESHUA. I speak Isaiah 32:15 over my life until the Spirit be poured upon Joshua, be poured upon my family, be poured upon my finances, be poured upon my destiny, be poured upon my business from on high, and let my wilderness be a fruitful field and the fruitful field be counted as a forest. Holy Ghost, there is a curse that is keeping me down. Holy Ghost, there is a curse that is keeping my finances down. Holy Ghost, there is a curse that is keeping my family down. In the mighty name of YESHUA, I hand you over to that curse, that familiar spirit that has taken away my glory and the glory of my family in my life. I hand you over to the Holy Ghost. Now, the Bible says there was darkness and the Holy Ghost hovered round the face of the deep.

So, dark disappointment, I hand you over to the Holy Ghost. I'm tired of carrying this pain. I'm tired of staying stagnant. I'm tired of not moving forward. I'm tired of being broke. I'm tired of carrying the shame. I'm tired of carrying this disappointment, this embargo over my head. Spirit of the Living God, I hand over my life in its entirety to you. I hand over the ministry. I hand over my business ideas. I hand over my pain. I hand over my sin. I hand over my addiction. You are a master over darkness, and I decree and I declare that I am yours to do with as you please. Mold me, shape me into the vessel you designed and created me to be in YESHUA's name. And it is so, it shall be so.

TESTIMONY# 15

Testimony:

For many years, my family and I struggled under the weight of unseen forces that seemed to hold us back. Despite our efforts, we faced repeated disappointments, financial struggles, and emotional pain. It felt as though there were curses and embargoes placed on our lives that prevented us from experiencing the fullness of God's blessings.

One night, in a moment of desperation and faith, I prayed this prayer, declaring Yeshua's name over every area of our lives. I handed over every curse, every familiar spirit, and every form of darkness to the Holy Ghost. I invited the Spirit of the Living God to take control and help us break free from the chains that bound us.

As I prayed, I felt a powerful shift in the atmosphere. It was as though a heavy burden was lifted from my shoulders. The Holy Spirit's presence was tangible, bringing peace and reassurance that God was at work in our situation. I declared Isaiah 32:15 over our lives, believing that the Spirit would transform our wilderness into a fruitful field.

In the weeks that followed, we began to see remarkable changes. The financial struggles that had weighed us down began to ease, and opportunities for growth and prosperity emerged. The emotional pain and disappointment were replaced with joy and hope. We experienced breakthroughs in areas that had been stagnant for years.

The most profound change was the renewed sense of purpose and direction. The Holy Spirit began to mold and shape us into the vessels

God designed us to be. We found strength in our faith, and our relationship with God deepened. The curses that had once held us back were broken, and we walked in the freedom and victory that Yeshua promised.

Today, I testify to the transformative power of the Holy Ghost. Our lives are a testament to God's faithfulness and the power of prayer. We no longer live under the shadow of curses and embargoes but in the light of God's grace and blessings. In Yeshua's name, it is so, and it shall be so.

ENOUGH IS ENOUGH PRAYER

Jehovah Nissi Sabaoth God above all flesh, Lord, you have brought me here today to lift me. I decree and I declare that the power of the Holy Ghost, the supernatural advantage, comes upon my life now in your atmosphere. I lie down in your presence. I ask you, to come speak to me, come be my friend, Lord, there are millions of people depending on this direction you have shown and given. What are you saying, Oh God? What are you saying, okay? Turn the place upside down. What is the secret behind the glory placed upon my life? Jehovah Raffi blow Like a mighty wind, blow away every sadness in my life, blow away every stagnation in my life, blow away every negative prophecy in my life, blow away every health issue in my life and my family's life. Lord, your word says I search for a man who will stand in the gap who will not destroy them. Help me, Father, to be that man. Enough is enough, if not for my sight for my children sake. I've gone through the pain already. Let innocent people not go through this again to me through my life through you in my life in Yeshua's Name. I've gone through the poverty. I've gone through the sickness. I've gone through the addictions. I went through the pain of idolatry. I went through the pain of altars plaguing me. I went through the pain of polygamy. I went through the pain of delay. I've gone through it for their sake! Use me to mold me in any way you see fit. Abba Father, teach me how to be an example. Teach me how to be a light for the sake of those connected to me. I decree and declare that I've made up my mind and I make a covenant with God, and everything I suffered in my life ends with me. My children will never go through what I went through, whether it's physical or spiritual. Send prayer advancement. Let it end with me. the poverty the failure the stagnation Satan, no further shall you go in my life or my familys life in the name of Yeshua. Every spirit that is not of God that has tied down my life or my family's life, I decree, and I declare that as I shout YESHUA, (then shout YESHUA) those spirits and devils leave me now. I am delivered now. My family is released from the devils of ancestry operations of covenants. I come by the blood of the Lamb. In the name of Yeshua, and I decree and I declare let me and my family go now! Release our destiny. Now I am released in the name of Yeshua from every form of oppression. Abba Father your word says now the Lord is that spirit and where the spirit of the Lord is there is liberty so I decree and I declare Yahweh is blotting out every handwriting and every word curse and every ordinance of darkness spoken against me and my family therefore I administer life and deliverance right now to myself and my family in the name of YESHUA myself and every one of my family members that is under siege where we don't rise or we don't Excel in the name of Yeshua of the fire rest upon me and my family now I release me and my family now, I release the year of 2024 unto me and my family I decree and I declare liberty by the spirit liberty by the spirit liberty by the spirit in the name of YESHUA right now the chain of delay in my life or my family life right now be broken be broken in JESUS Name and it is so!

TESTIMONY# 16

Testimony:

There was a time in my life when everything seemed to be falling apart. Every effort I made was met with resistance, and the weight of shame and failure was overwhelming. I felt trapped in a cycle of defeat and despair. It was during this time that I discovered the power of declaring God's promises over my life.

I began to decree and declare victory, healing, and restoration in the name of Jesus. With each declaration, I felt a shift in my spirit. The heavy burdens began to lift, and I started to see breakthroughs in areas where I had previously faced only obstacles. My health improved, relationships were restored, and opportunities that had once seemed out of reach became attainable.

One of the most profound changes was the transformation in my mindset. I moved from a place of doubt and defeat to one of faith and expectancy. I witnessed firsthand the power of speaking life into my circumstances and aligning my words with God's promises.

Today, I can confidently say that the Lord has raised me from the dust of shame and decorated my life with His favor and blessings. This prayer has been a cornerstone in my journey towards freedom and victory, and I am forever grateful for the power of faith-filled declarations.

Prayer For Demonic Headaches

In Jesus' name, I decree and declare every Spirit troubling me must leave now and every condition that is in partnership with any Spirit, mocking God in my life, I arrest you now; you must go. I decree and declare that I receive Grace. Any area where I have failed in the past, I go back and produce results now in Jesus' name. Hallelujah! Anything that is discomforting me, that devil must leave now, that Spirit must leave now in Jesus' name. Restoration, come now in the name of Jesus Christ. By the power of the raised Christ from the dead, may God raise me from the dust of shame finally, raise me from the dust of shame and decorate my life like Pharaoh did Joseph Amen in the name of Jesus Christ, place upon my head favor and blessings that which even in prison the king can send for me and bring me out of any dungeon in the name of Jesus. Place upon my life that grace and favor that when someone shakes my hand, they shake hands with favor they shake hands with speed they shake hands with breakthrough. Anything in my life that is not working in the name of Jesus, I decree and declare that it begins to work now, Lord, I'm tired of the shame & reproach over myself over my family and over my loved ones why is it that good thing keep happening until I show up and then the narrative just changes there is a way out I don't know what the way is but I know there's a way out I engage by faith in Jesus name indeed it is my day God has given me a story whatever disease or infirmity that may have been plaguing me is leaving, finally the cycle of shame and reproach backwardness retrogression is giving way in the name of Jesus. It's time for gates to be open, it's time for doors to be open now, time for new chapters to be open, engage my faith, open supernatural favor, awaken in me supernatural faith now. I decree and declare in Jesus name that every spirit that is keeping me and everybody around me poor and limited in any way or begging and incertitude in the name of Jesus, I curse you by the spirit of GOD. Many things in our lives are connected with empowerment, many things in our lives will make progress when prayer and empowerment are at work with in us. In the name of Jesus any sickness any kind of body limitation, smallness in life, or in Destiny & poverty wreaking havoc in my life, I curse you and arrest you by the spirit of the living God. In the name of Jesus, the spirit where you achieve things but they never last, I arrest you and cancel you by the spirit of the Living God. I decree and declare everything that is causing me to go up and then come down and not stay up, I am delivered right now this moment, I'm delivered right now this moment in the name of Jesus, and any rising only to go down by the spirit of the Living God whether it's for me or my family, that fire, let it bring a separation on that Spirit forever between me and the spirit forever. I'm separated now and forever in the name of Jesus Christ. I decree and declare right now by the power of the Holy Spirit in the name of Jesus. May the hand of God rest upon me now. May the hand of God rest upon me, now every demonic headache masquerading as any recurring headache, I decree and declare I am healed now and any eye condition total or temporary blindness, by the power of the Holy Ghost, I began to see now. Any conditions where it's hard to move my legs, I'm here right now. I'm able to do what I couldn't do before, right now in Jesus' name. The pain goes back now and it is to be healed now. Shoulder pain is to be healed now, neck pain is to be healed now, and in the name of JESUS, healing in life comes now. Any heart conditions, high blood pressure, anything if it was not so, in the beginning, let it be so now in Jesus' name, I am healed. In the name of Jesus anything that is holding me or plaguing me or keeping me down in any way, I decree and declare the Lord is raising Me from the bed of languishing now. I'm healed from any kidney conditions, any conditions where if I bend in any kind of way, I am in morbid pain. Let that pain disappear now in the name of Jesus Christ. The condition where there is pain or problems in my toes, the power of God is touching me and healing me right now in the name of Jesus. In the name of Jesus, let a visitation come for me and my family members, any conditions where I eat a little food and I throw up and I'm sick anything that is related to the devil must leave me now in Jesus' name. Any arthritic or mobility problems in the name that is above all names the pain goes now and I decree and declare my season has come because the Lord is taking away arrows of witchcraft. I decree and declare I am delivered now by the spirit of the Living God. Every Spirit of witchcraft around me, or my family, I decree and declare, I am delivered now and my family is delivered now in the name of Jesus Christ Jehovah Nissi. I decree declare that you will relocate me to wherever you want me to have a new chapter in ministry in life in the name of Jesus, open a new chapter in life and ministry for me by the power of the Holy Ghost multiply my visions. I received Grace now I received accuracy in my perception from this day forth. Lord, I submit my prayer to your will and to your word in JESUS Name and it is so it shall be so!

TESTIMONY# 17

Testimony:

There was a time in my life when I felt overwhelmed by the afflictions and challenges that came my way. Despite my faith and efforts, I encountered numerous setbacks and difficulties. It was during this period that I realized I needed to seek a deeper understanding and break free from any spiritual hindrances affecting my life.

One night, I prayed this prayer with a fervent heart, seeking the intervention of Yeshua. I declared that every mind-binding spirit, every form of witchcraft, and every negative decree over my life would be broken. I spoke scriptures over my life, affirming that I am blessed coming in and going out, that I have the mind of Christ, and that I am filled with God's wisdom and understanding.

As I prayed, I felt a profound sense of liberation and peace. The burdens that had weighed me down began to lift. In the days that followed, I noticed significant changes. The clarity of mind I had longed for returned, and the spirit of fear and anxiety was replaced with a deep sense of peace and assurance.

Physically, I experienced healing and restoration. The ailments that had plagued me were alleviated, and I felt a renewed sense of vitality. Emotionally and spiritually, I was strengthened, and my faith grew stronger. I found myself walking in the supernatural wisdom of God, able to navigate life's challenges with newfound confidence.

This prayer marked a turning point in my life. The power of God's word and the authority in Yeshua's name brought about a transformation that I had never experienced before. I am grateful for the total grace and power of obedience that God granted me. Today, I live in the freedom, peace, and wholeness that only God can provide.

I continue to declare God's promises over my life and pray for others who are in need of healing and deliverance. My life is a testament to the faithfulness of God and the power of prayer. In Yeshua's name, it is so, and it shall be so.

Prayer For Healing Upon Yourself

The name of YESHUA gives me understanding even by Your word many are the afflictions of the righteous, the righteous businessman, the righteous apostle, the righteous prophet, the righteous mother, the righteous student, the righteous politician, and even the righteous Nation when the afflictions come upon me, teach Me to look to you YESHUA in your name. I decree and I declare that my life will begin to be so accurate because I will function within the confines of the ways of Yahweh. In the mighty name of YESHUA, I break every mind-binding spirit off my life now. I decree and I declare the power of witchcraft is broken over my life in the name of YESHUA. I command every lie, and false decree spell an incantation to be broken over my life now in Yeshua's name. All witchcraft attacks upon my life go now I command every mind binding Spirit to loose me and go now in the name of Yeshua I speak Deuteronomy 28:6 over my life now I am blessed coming in and I am blessed going out. Every curse over my life or my family's life falls under the power of the blood of Yeshua. I decree and I declare that I have a sound mind from this day forth. I think only God's thoughts, I dream only God's dreams, I imagine only godly imaginations, I speak Philippians 2:5 over my life now I have the mind of Christ; I am saturated and peace and protection, I decree it and I declare that I walk in the supernatural wisdom of God I speak proverbs 2:6 over my life now the Lord has provided me with wisdom knowledge and understanding I have a sound mind I am free from the spirit of fear and In Yeshua's name, I hear clearly, I see clearly, I think clearly, and I walk clearly, I am free abba father. I thank You for Your Love, Peace, and, freedom over my life now I worship you and praise you that I am free in my mind. In the name of Yeshua and it is so it shall be so! Abba Father, I ask for the Total Grace for power for my Total obedience that in all you demand me to do, make good your word. I obtain Grace in Yeshua Name. I decree and declare by grace I obtain true faith; I am lifted by grace. I decree and declare; I am rising by grace. True Faith is my action of obedience, I come before you today to heal my body, mind, and Spirit.

I decree & I declare that I am a child of God, and I have been given the power to bind every negative spiritual force that may be causing sickness, disease, or infirmity in my life and to loose every positive spiritual force that can bring healing, restoration, and wholeness to every area of my life.

I bind every Spirit of sickness, disease, and infirmity that may be causing pain and suffering in my body.

I command every negative medical report or diagnosis to be nullified.

I lose the Spirit of healing, restoration, and wholeness that can bring health and wellness to every area of my life.

I also bind every Spirit of fear, anxiety, and worry that may be causing me to doubt your healing power and to live in a state of emotional distress.

I loose the Spirit of peace, comfort, and hope that could bring emotional healing and stability to my life. I declare that the blood of Jesus covers me, and I command every negative spiritual force to flee from my body, mind, and Spirit.

I thank you, God, for your healing power, love, and mercy, and I receive every healing you have in store for me

I also pray for those suffering from illness and disease that they, too, would experience your healing power and receive the physical, emotional, and spiritual healing they need.

In Jesus' name, & it is so.

TESTIMONY# 18

Testimony:

There was a time when it felt like everything in my life was under attack. My health, my family, my finances, and my destiny seemed to be targeted by forces that brought nothing but shame, delay, and reproach. I was left bound by invisible chains, unable to make the progress I knew God had destined for me.

One night, I prayed this prayer with all the faith I could muster. I declared the power of Yeshua over every spirit assigned to bring me down. I raised a standard by the blood of Jesus, breaking every curse and yoke of delay. I stood as a priest and intercessor for my family, declaring release and liberty over each one of us.

As I prayed, I felt a tangible shift in the atmosphere. It was as if the heavy burdens that had weighed me down were being lifted. The presence of the Holy Spirit filled the room, and I knew that God was at work. In the days and weeks that followed, I began to see significant changes. The delays and setbacks that had plagued us were removed. Opportunities that had been blocked suddenly opened up.

By health improved, and the chronic ailments that had troubled me were heated. My family's relationships were restored, and there was a newfound peace in our home. Financial breakthroughs came, and we experienced God's provision in ways we had never seen before. The spirit of fear and anxiety was replaced with boldness and confidence.

This prayer marked a turning point in my life. The power of Yeshua and the authority of His name brought about a complete transformation. I am now walking in the freedom, victory, and blessing that God intended for me. I continue to stand on His promises, knowing that He who began a good work in me will carry it on to completion.

Today, I testify to the goodness and faithfulness of God. He has broken every chain, healed every wound, and restored every lost blessing. My life is a testament to the power of prayer and the victory we have in Yeshua. In His name, it is so, and it shall be so.

Prayer For Unclean Spirits

The name of YESHUA, every spirit assigned over my Life and over my destiny, my ministry, my family, my mind, my loins, my spirit, my health, brings me shame and reproach in this end time. I raise a standard by the blood, I raise a standard by the blood 5x. In the name of Yeshua, anybody who plants anything evil around my life or my family life, beginning this night the earth will bury them. ABBA Father in the name of Yeshua, I take authority over every influence over every spirit assigned to my life and assigned to my destiny. I stand in the victory of Yeshua and I establish it in my life now, establishing victory through understanding, establishing victory by faith, establishing victory by spiritual intelligence, in Yeshua name, Jehovah nissi. Myself & every member of my family who's in bondage now I stand as a priest and I stand as an intercessor and I decree and I declare by the blood of Yeshua, I am released now, they are released now, not under my watch, release me now, release them now by the blood in the name of YESHUA Jehovah Ralpha. I decree and I declare that the fullness of my days, I will fulfill!! Every assignment of hell to take my Life before my time or to take the Life of my Loved ones before their time is cancelled now. I decree and I declare in the Air and protected on the land, I am protected by the sea. I decree and I declare any kidnapper any driver or anyone who tries to come at a son or a daughter of Zion, made my God judge them instantly in the name of Yeshua. Anyone who means evil for me and my loved ones I am praying by the spirit; may my God judge them. Any demonic presence or spirits must leave me tonight, any demonic atmosphere must leave me tonight and in the name of Yeshua, everything that does not represent God in my life must leave tonight. In the name of Yeshua, the son of the Living, God every High thing in my life must come down every stronghold shall be broken now. Anywhere in my life where my destiny has been tied down or delayed where I would not make progress. In the name of Yeshua, I am declaring right the Yoke of delay is broken now by the spirit of the Living God and I decree and I declare that Grace is falling on me now, and the yoke of delay is broken over my life right now. I rebuke delay in my life, I rebuke the lay over my ministry, I rebuke delay over my finances for the power that raised Yeshua from the grave. I'm set free now I prophesy restoration. I decree and declare Liberty from delay in the name of YESHUA. I curse foundations and every covenant of ancestry whatever yoke of darkness. By the word of the Lord, I am set free now, my family is set so I Decree and I declare bring me liberty now Liberty by the spirit in Jesus name. I come against anything that represents the beast plaguing myself or any one of my family tied to witchcraft. I am delivered right now, my family is delivered right now, anything in my life or my family's life that is not of God that is tied me or my family to the devil every evil that is not of God because it's not been planted by GOD Let It Be uprooted now. let it be uprooted from my life now everything that represents the workings of darkness or the workings of witchcraft let it be broken now from my life, from my family 's life, from my destiny never to return again in the Yeshua's Name. Oh my God! raise me for the sake of my loved ones and to be a threat to the ministry of darkness. May God bless me to be a blessing to others in the name of Jesus Christ. The grace for apostolic leadership, may it rest upon me now and in the name of Yeshua the dealings of the spirit that will make me become a powerful vessel of God, may that Grace come up on me now. Any new covenant connected to me or my family that kills people and destroys people in the name of Yeshua, I decree and I declare that spirit leaves me and my family once and for all and everything that is missing from my life. I decree and I declare that is being restored right now by the power that raised Christ from the dead.

TESTIMONY# 19

Testimony:

There was a time when it felt like everything in my life was under attack. My health, my family, my finances, and my destiny seemed to be targeted by forces that brought nothing but shame, delay, and reproach. I felt bound by invisible chains, unable to make the progress I knew God had destined for me.

One night, I prayed this prayer with all the faith I could muster. I declared the power of Yeshua over every spirit assigned to bring me down. I raised a standard by the blood of Jesus, breaking every curse and yoke of delay. I stood as a priest and intercessor for my family, declaring release and liberty over each one of us.

As I prayed, I felt a tangible shift in the atmosphere. It was as if the heavy burdens that had weighed me down were being lifted. The presence of the Holy Spirit filled the room, and I knew that God was at work. In the days and weeks that followed, I began to see significant changes. The delays and setbacks that had plagued us were removed. Opportunities that had been blocked suddenly opened up.

My health improved, and the chronic ailments that had troubled me were healed. My family's relationships were restored, and there was a newfound peace in our home. Financial breakthroughs came, and we experienced God's provision in ways we had never seen before. The spirit of fear and anxiety was replaced with boldness and confidence.

This prayer marked a turning point in my life. The power of Yeshua and the authority of His name brought about a complete transformation.

I am now walking in the freedom, victory, and blessing that God intended for me. I continue to stand on His promises, knowing that He who began a good work in me will carry it on to completion,

Today, I testify to the goodness and faithfulness of God. He has broken every chain, healed every wound, and restored every lost blessing. My life is a testament to the power of prayer and the victory we have in Yeshua. In His name, it is so, and it shall be so.

PRAYER FOR FORBID GOING BACK TO THE OLD ME.

Lord, your word says "Now, therefore, proclaim in the hearing of the people saying whoever is fearful and afraid let him turn and depart at once from Mount Gilead and 22,000 of the people returned and 10,000 remained Judges" 7:3. In the mighty name of Yeshua, I forbid returning back to the old me over my Life. I decree and I Declare I will pass this test, In the name of Yeshua. I conquer fear, the fear of opinions, the fear of failure, the fear of the past, the fear of the future in the name of Yeshua. I conquer fear, the fear of tomorrow, and the fear over my destiny. I decree and I declare the Lord is with me, standing by me like a mighty terrible warrior in the name of Yeshua. I decree and declare the grace comes upon my life. The mantle where when people look at me and say I used to know You, I can say 'yes' but not that version anymore, fix me. Oh God! Work on me oh God! Abba Father what does it take for my glory to rise and fix me? If it takes fasting, fix me God, if it takes prayer, fix Me Elohim, if it takes me going for training, fix it Yahweh, if it takes another level of education and knowledge, fix Me Jehovah Nissi but by all means, I refuse to remain Ordinary, by all means I refuse to remain a mediocre. By all Abba Father, why is it that every time I start good things something evil must come for the sake of me and my family. Oh GOD! Arise oh God! That ride's upon the wings of the wind Arise I tear down any Altars plaguing me Tonight, I use prayer as a system of authorization this bad luck upon my Life must stop, This Yoke must be broken now in the name of Yeshua. Tonight, I stand on behalf of myself

and my family and I decree and I declare that every altar that is speaking
against my destiny, I tear it down tonight, I tear it down Altars of Delay,
Altars of Barrenness, Altars of Failure, I tear it down in Yeshua's Name.
In the name of Jesus Every legal access I have given any Altar to speak
against me knowingly and unknowingly tonight I invoke the blood let
the blood speak in Yeshua 's Name and It Is So!

TESTIMONY# 20

Testimony:

There was a period in my life when Tears and unseen altars seemed to have a grip on every aspect of my existence. The fear of opinions, failure, the past, and the future kept me bound, preventing me from progressing and achieving the destiny God had set for me. Each time I attempted to start something good, evil seemed to arise, blocking my path.

One night, I prayed this prayer with determination and faith, refusing to return to the old me. I declared victory over every fear and commanded every spirit of delay, barrenness, and failure to be torn down. As I invoked the power of the blood of Yeshua, I felt an overwhelming sense of peace and assurance that God was at work.

In the days that followed, significant changes began to manifest. The Tears that once held me captive lost their power. I faced situations with newfound courage and confidence, knowing that the Lord was with me like a mighty warrior. People who knew me remarked on the transformation they saw, and I could boldly affirm that I was no longer the person I used to be.

The altars that had spoken against my destiny were broken. Opportunities that had been blocked opened up, and I experienced breakthroughs in various areas of my life. The cycle of bad luck and setbacks was broken, and I walked in the favor and blessings of God.

My journey to rising above mediocrity and embracing the extraordinary purpose God has for me continues. Through fasting, prayer, and seeking further education and training, I am continually being shaped into the vessel God designed me to be. Each step forward is a testament to His grace and power.

Today, I stand as a living testimony of God's transformative power. The fears and altars that once bound me are no more, and I walk in freedom and victory. My life is a testament to the power of prayer, the blood of Yeshua, and the unwavering faithfulness of God. In Yeshua's name, it is so, and it shall be so.